About the Author

ARTHUR STECKLER was a combat cameraman in the U.S. Marine Corps, after which he went to work in the motion picture industry as assistant director, director, and production manager. He has worked on all kinds of films, from *On the Waterfront* to eight-second commercials. In the course of his service and civilian careers, Mr. Steckler has traveled extensively, and the various languages he has encountered have sharpened his interest in word origins.

Mr. Steckler now divides his time between writing and making motion pictures. He and his wife and two daughters live in New London, Connecticut.

About the Artist

JAMES FLORA, the well-known illustrator and art director, has had his drawings published in many major U.S. magazines and has written and illustrated fifteen children's books as well.

Mr. Flora attended and later worked at the Cincinnati Art Academy and, after a stint as a mural painter, founded Little Man Press with Robert Lowry. Subsequently he has been an art director, free-lance illustrator, and writer. Mr. Flora, his wife, and their five children now live in Rowayton, Connecticut.

101 words

and how they began

by Arthur Steckler

Drawings by James Flora

Doubleday & Company, Inc.
Garden City, New York

sniffle

Library of Congress Catalog Card Number 78-1012
ISBN 0-385-14073-8 Trade
ISBN 0-385-14074-6 Prebound
Text copyright © 1979 by Arthur Steckler
Illustrations copyright © 1979 by James Flora

For Lisa and Erika,
and the other
neighborhood critics

buzz   shriek   chatter   hiccup   sneeze   rattle   sn...

The words we use have come from many different sources. Some of them came from languages thousands of years old. Others came from some of the almost three thousand different languages that are spoken today around the world.

Some words came to us from slang, others from the Bible or from science. Some came from the initials of other words.

There are words that came from sounds or noises, like *giggle*, and *gargle*, and *gurgle*, and *rattle*, and *chatter*, and *tinkle*, and *hiccup*, and *bubble*, and *shriek*, and *buzz*, and *slam*, and *pop*. If you've ever heard a door *slam*, or a balloon *pop*, you might agree that these words certainly sound like what happened. They are called *onomatopoetic* or *onomatopoeic* words, which is a fancy way to say, "making words by the sound of the action involved."

There are words that came from the place where a thing was first used, such as: *dungarees*, *cantaloupe*, and *dollar*.

There are some words that are strange for other reasons. *Sniff* and *sniffle* and *snuff* and *snuffle* and *snout* and *snort* and *sneeze* are all words that describe the nose and its activities. For some strange reason, all begin with the letters *sn*. No one really knows why.

There are even words which are mistakes, but which we use anyway, like *kangaroo* and *turkey*.

If you were to read that "a catta pilosa was crawling on the tooth of a lion when a man of the forest had him clear away the table," it wouldn't make much sense. But if you knew that a "catta pilosa" was a caterpillar, that the "tooth of a lion" was a dandelion, that "a man of the forest" was an orangutan, and that the definition of dessert was to "clear away the table," then the same sentence would read, "A caterpillar was crawling on a dandelion when an orangutan had him for dessert," which makes more sense to the reader, and maybe to the orangutan, but certainly not to the caterpillar.

If you have the letter *C* on one of your water faucets, it stands for "cold" in English-speaking countries. But in France, Spain, and Italy, it stands for "hot," because the French word

for hot is *chaud,* the Spanish word for hot is *caliente,* and the Italian word for hot is *caldo.* (So if you visit France, Spain, or Italy, be careful when you turn on the cold water faucet, or you'll find yourself in hot water.)

A name is a word by which a person, place, or thing is known. And just as words can have interesting beginnings, so can names.

Giuseppe Verdi was a famous composer of music. If you translate his Italian name into English, it becomes just plain Joseph Green, because Giuseppe is the Italian for Joseph, and Verdi is the Italian for Green.

Probably the most common masculine name is John. Yet as we go from country to country and language to language, see how it changes:

Italy	Giovanni
Turkey	Yuhanna
Spain	Juan
Ireland	Sean
Denmark	Jens
France	Jean
Brazil	Joaninho
Morocco	Yahya
Switzerland	Johann
India	Zaid
Holland	Jan
Greece	Ioannes
Thailand	Yohan
Japan	Yohana-den
Russia	Ivan
Austria	Hansel

If you asked an airline agent for a ticket from "Red Stick" to "White House," there's no telling what he might think, or where you might end up. But if you knew that Baton Rouge, the city in Louisiana, when translated from French to English, becomes "Red Stick," and that Casablanca, in Morocco, when translated from Spanish to English, becomes "White House," you would at least know where you were going, even if you didn't want to go there.

There are many, many words that seem to play tricks or games on us.

Words About People

kindergarten

Let's start with the word KINDERGARTEN. In the German language, the word for child is *Kind,* which rhymes with *pinned.* The word for children is *Kinder.* Now, if you take the German word for garden, which is *Garten,* and add the word *Kinder* to it, you have the word KINDERGARTEN. In the German language, that means "a garden of children," which is certainly what a KINDERGARTEN suggests to most people.

acrobat

If you went to the circus, you would probably see some ACROBATS and CLOWNS. What you might not know is that the word ACROBAT is from the French language by way of the Greek word *akros,* which means "at the point, end, or top of." It literally means "one who walks on tiptoe." Except for a lot of tumbling, that's pretty much what an ACROBAT does.

clown

CLOWN is a word that comes from three Scandinavian countries: Sweden, Denmark, and Iceland, and possibly the Dutch or German languages. Their words *klunn* and *klunni* mean a clumsy or clownish fellow. That pretty much describes how a clown acts.

barber

The word BARBER was originally a Latin word *barba,* which means "beard." The French borrowed the word, and it became *barbe.* We borrowed it, and it became BARBER, someone who takes care of hair and beards. The BARBER pole, with its spiral stripes of red and white, represents a bandage covering a bleeding limb. It goes back to the days when BARBERS did more surgery than trimming of hair and beards.

butler

Just as a BARBER takes his name from beards, a BUTLER takes his name from bottles. In old England, the word *bottle* used to be spelled *botel,* and a *boteler* was a person who attended to botels. Today, one of the jobs of a BUTLER is to serve drinks from bottles, though he does other things. In olden France, there was a person called a *bouteillier,* who was a cupbearer, which is pretty much what a BUTLER does.

doctor

Some words have very direct beginnings, such as the word DOCTOR. DOCTOR is from the Latin word *doctor,* which means "teacher." Since a DOCTOR of dentistry, or dentist, teaches us how to care for our teeth, and a medical DOCTOR teaches us about health, it is easy to see how DOCTOR means teacher.

bandit

When we think of BANDIT, we usually think of the old West. Yet the word BANDIT started out as the German word *Bann,* which meant "a summons," and a Latin word *bannire,* meaning "to banish" or "proscribe." *Bannire* became the Italian word *bandito,* which referred to something or someone "outlawed." We changed the word to BANDIT, and kept the meaning "outlawed" or "outlaw."

sheriff

In western movies, the person who usually follows a BANDIT is the SHERIFF. SHERIFF is from an early English word, or actually from two early English words. The word *shire* (as in Hampshire) means a "province." The word *reeve* means an "officer" or "steward." By putting them together, we get *shire-reeve,* or SHERIFF.

slave

The words SLAVE and ROBOT have somewhat similar beginnings. The Slavic people of Central Europe—Russians, Czechoslovakians, Poles, and so on—known as "Slavs," were once conquered and put into slavery. With regular usage, the word changed from *Slav* to SLAVE.

robot

ROBOT is from the Czechoslovakian word *robotnik,* which means "slave." This came from an earlier word *robota,* meaning "service" or "work." *Robota* is related to and sounds like the German word for work, *Arbeit,* which is what slaves were forced to do. Even though SLAVE and ROBOT are two entirely different words, it is interesting to see how the words' meanings have intertwined.

Santa Claus

Unless you speak Dutch, you have probably never heard of anyone named Sinterklaas. But in Old Holland, the patron saint of children was St. Nikolaas, or Nicholas. The Dutch name for St. Nicholas is Sinterklaas. If you say the name Sinterklaas several times, it soon starts to sound like SANTA CLAUS. The Dutch language and the Dutch name Sinterklaas, as you can see, are where we get our name SANTA CLAUS.

Words About th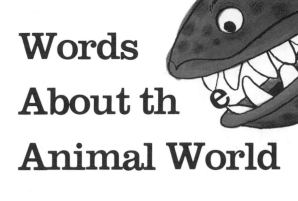e Animal World

dinosaur

Two animals, both from olden times, one that is extinct and another that still exists, are named after lizards. The name of the extinct one, the DINOSAUR, came from the language of the ancient Greeks. Their words *deinos,* which means "fearful," and *sauros,* which means "lizard," were combined to name the fearful lizard known as the DINOSAUR.

alligator

ALLIGATORS, which of course still exist, were also named after lizards, but their name came from Latin to Spanish, and eventually to English. Early Spanish settlers, when they first saw an ALLIGATOR, called it *el lagarto,* which meant "the lizard," or "the great lizard." *El lagarto* later became *alligarta.* When it entered the English language, it became ALLIGATOR, which is what it remains today.

poodle

If you had a POODLE PUPPY, you would have a pet that got its name from two languages, in interesting ways. The word POODLE comes from the German word *Pudel*, which comes from *Pudelhund,* meaning "splash-hound." *Pudeln* meant "to splash in water," and *Hund* meant "hound" or "dog." So POODLE originally meant "splash-hound," and strangely enough, the words *Pudel* and *puddle* come from the same word source. It's easy to see how a *Pudel* might enjoy splashing in a puddle, which is really how that dog got its name. So, if anyone tells you it's raining cats and dogs, don't step in a "poodle"—you really know what they mean.

puppy

The word PUPPY is from the French word *poupée,* which means "little doll," or "baby." So a PUPPY is really a little baby dog, even if he's not French and even if he's not a POODLE.

rhinoceros

The names of two rather large animals also have unusual beginnings. The RHINOCEROS got its name from the ancient Greek language. The Greek word for nose was *rhinos*, while the Greek word for horn was *keras.* By putting these words together, we get *rhinoskeras,* meaning "nose-horn." Down through the years, *rhinoskeras* became RHINOCEROS, that big, big animal with a horn on its nose.

hippopotamus

HIPPOPOTAMUS also came to us from two ancient Greek words, *hippos,* which means a "horse," and *potamos,* which means a "river." So a HIPPOPOTAMUS was really a "river horse," according to the Greek and then the Latin languages. When talking about two or more of these animals, some people say "hippopotamuses" and some say "hippopotami." It's probably fair to say that the decision should really be left up to the animals themselves.

walrus

Just as HIPPOPOTAMUS meant "river horse," the name WALRUS originally meant "whale-horse," but in a completely different language. The Danish people, when they first saw a WALRUS, thought it looked a bit like a whale and a bit like a horse. They named it a *hvalros,* or "whale-horse." *Hvalros* became WALRUS, and that's how words enter our language.

mosquito

Going from very big to very small members of the animal kingdom, we find the word MOSQUITO. The Latin word *musca* and the Spanish and Portugese word *mosca* both mean a fly. By adding *ito* to the end of *mosca,* it became a little fly. The name of the capital of Ecuador is Quito, from the Quitu Indians of that area. Since Ecuador got its name from the hot, steamy equator, where it is situated, and where there must be many mosquitoes, it seems fitting that the name of the capital and the word MOSQUITO are so similar.

turkey

Two birds we find in America have interesting names. An old legend tells us that the bird we eat on Thanksgiving was named after the country of Turkey, but was named by mistake. The first settlers who came to America saw a bird that reminded them of a bird from Turkey. They named the American bird TURKEY, even though the story tells us that it was later found to be an entirely different kind of bird.

flamingo

Another interesting bird, the brightly colored FLAMINGO, took its name from the Latin word *flamma,* which means flame. If we remove the letter *o* from FLAMINGO, we get *flaming,* and we realize that the name for this bird was based on its most identifiable feature, its fiery color.

porcupine

If someone told us that the PORCUPINE was a prickly pig, we would probably agree, and we should, because that's what its name means. The French word *porc,* which means "pig" or "hog," was combined with *d'espine,* which means "spine" or "prickle." When the word came into the English language, it was changed from *porc d'espine* to *porkepyn* and eventually became PORCUPINE.

orangutan

Even the country of Malaya in Southeast Asia and the Malayan language gave us some of our language. Their word *oran* means "man." Their word *utan* means "of the forest." By combining them, we get ORANGUTAN, which means "man of the forest." If you've ever seen an ORANGUTAN, you'll agree that nothing describes him better than that.

caterpillar

Even the little CATERPILLAR got its name in a strange way. In Latin, the word for "cat" is *catta;* the word for "hair" is *pilosa.* Put them together, and the result is *catta pilosa,* which means "hairy cat." If the next

CATERPILLAR you see looks like a hairy cat, then the Latin language, the French language, and now the English language agree with you.

kangaroo

An interesting story is told about the Australian KANGAROO. Once, a visitor to that far-off land asked a native the name of that animal. The native, known as an Aborigine, replied, "KANGAROO," thereby naming the animal for the visitor. Later, it was found that the word KANGAROO meant "I don't know."

Words About Things That Grow

tulip

When people think of TULIPS, most of them think of the Netherlands. But they should think of Turkey, Italy, and France, because those are the countries that brought us the name TULIP. Long ago, in the country of Turkey, people thought the flower looked like the turban that most Turkish men wore as a headpiece. The word for turban was *tulbend*. From *tulbend* to TULIP was simply a matter of time, from the Turkish *tulbend,* to the Italian *tulipano,* to the French *tulipan,* and finally to the English word TULIP.

dandelion

The DANDELION got its name because some Frenchman had a pretty good imagination. He imagined that the leaf of the plant looked like the tooth of a lion. When we translate "tooth of the lion" into French, it becomes "dent de lion." It was only a matter of time before "dent de lion" became DANDELION.

daisy

Another little wild flower, the DAISY got its name from the early English language. From the Anglo-Saxon *daeges eage,* it changed to the Middle English *dayesye.*

These meant the "day's eye," or the "eye of the day": that is, the sun. Since the petals of the DAISY open during the day and close at night, as the sun appears and disappears, it's easy to see how the DAISY was given its name.

pineapple

Another word from Middle English is PINEAPPLE. This word once meant "pine cone," the fruit of the pine tree, because *apple* could mean other kinds of fruit. To some people, the PINEAPPLE looked like a large pine cone, so that's how it got its name. In the German and French languages, the word for PINEAPPLE is *Ananas,* which sounds almost like *bananas,* which PINEAPPLES certainly are not.

shamrock

March 17, St. Patrick's Day, is known for the "wearing of the green." The "green," of course, refers to the SHAMROCK. The name of this little green plant came from the Gaelic word *seamrog,* which means "little clover." By the time *seamrog* found its way into the English language, it became SHAM-ROCK.

potato

Another plant that most people associate with Ireland is the
POTATO. Yet this word came to us from Haiti, by way of
Spain. The Haitian word for a kind of sweet potato known as a
yam is *batata*. This was changed by the Spanish to *patata,* and
our word is now POTATO.

cantaloupe

Long ago, on one of the Pope's country estates near Rome, a
certain type of melon was first grown. The town was called
Cantalupo, and the melons, after a trip through the Italian and·
French languages, were called CANTALOUPES.

tangerine

Legend tells us that the fruit we know as TANGERINE came to
us by way of Tangier in Morocco, and so it became a *tangier-
ine,* or TANGERINE. And even though it may seem strange, the
people who live in the city of Tangier are often called
TANGERINES.

Words About Things We Eat and Drink

hamburger

If you think the word HAMBURGER comes to us from Hamburg, Germany, you're right, just as frankfurters are named for Frankfurt, Germany. Originally the HAMBURGER was known as a Hamburg steak, and it was introduced to this country in 1884 when numbers of German settlers came to the United States.

ketchup

When we think of HAMBURGERS, we usually think of KETCHUP. Yet they come from completely different origins. Long ago in China, the Chinese people enjoyed a pickled fish sauce, which they called *ke-tsiap*. Over the years, this sauce changed, and so did its name, which became *kechap* in the Malayan language. Soon *kechap* became KETCHUP.

spaghetti

When we think of a bowlful of little cords or threads, we might think of a bowl of SPAGHETTI, and that is exactly how SPAGHETTI got its name. In Italy, the Italian word *spago* means a "small cord or thread." *Spaghetto* means a "thin thread." Thus, *spaghetto* or the plural SPAGHETTI became the name of that dish.

pretzel

A food that got its name from Germany is the PRETZEL. The German word *Prezel* or *Brezel* came from the Latin *brachium*, meaning "arm." (A *braccialetto*, in Italian, is a bracelet.) Also, *pretium* is Latin for "reward," and in the sixteenth century, monks used to give glazed cakes to children when they learned their prayers. It may be that the twisted shape of the PRETZEL represented the folded arms of the monks. Since these cakes were a reward, they were given the name *pretiola*, or "little rewards." The shape of the PRETZEL stayed the same, but the name changed from *pretiola* to PRETZEL.

cereal

In ancient Rome, there were many gods and goddesses. One of these, the goddess Ceres, was considered to be the protector of the crops, such as corn, or wheat. The corn or wheat CEREAL that we eat for breakfast was named after the goddess Ceres.

waffle

Whenever we pour syrup on a WAFFLE, we are pouring syrup on a Dutch word and a Dutch invention. Many years ago, in the Netherlands, someone invented the WAFFLE. They called it a *wafel,* which was the Dutch word for "wafer." When the *wafel* came to this country, the name came along, too, except that on the way it changed from *wafel* to WAFFLE.

coleslaw

Another Dutch word is COLESLAW. The Dutch word *kool* means "cabbage," and the Dutch word *sla* means "salad." It's pretty plain that COLESLAW is cabbage salad.

delicatessen

When we think of COLESLAW, we often think of DELICATESSEN. This German-sounding word is actually from the French word *délicatesse,* which means "delicacy." The German plural of the word is DELICATESSEN.

coffee

We get our word COFFEE from the Turkish and Arabic languages. *Qahveh* is the Turkish word for COFFEE, just as *qahwah* is the Arabic. Later, the French called it *café*. Their word for COFFEE also became their word for a coffee shop. *Café* became our word *cafeteria*, which, of course, is a self-service restaurant, although *cafeteria* comes from the Mexican Spanish *cafeteria*.

vinegar

VINEGAR is a word from the Old French language. The words *vin egre* meant "wine that was sour," or "sour wine." If you have ever tasted sour wine, you will see how VINEGAR got its name.

lollipop

When we eat a LOLLIPOP, we usually lick it with our tongue, which is probably how the word came into being. The northern English dialect word for tongue is *lolly*. This came from the word *loll,* which meant "to hang out the tongue." For some reason, the word *pop* was added to *lolly,* giving us the word for candy on a stick, the LOLLIPOP.

chocolate

When most people think of CHOCOLATE, they think of sweetness. So it might be surprising to know that the Mexican word *chocolatl* means "bitter water." But unsweetened CHOCOLATE is quite bitter, as the early Mexicans must have discovered when they first used CHOCOLATE to make beverages.

sandwich

John Montagu, the fourth Earl of Sandwich, in England, lived in the 1700s. He was so fond of gambling, it is said, that, rather than leave the gambling tables to eat his meals, he had his servants bring him meat between pieces of bread, something which was not common at that time. It is from the Earl of Sandwich that we got our word SANDWICH, according to this old legend.

dessert

Now that we have sampled all these food and beverages, what is left? DESSERT. But the word DESSERT might surprise you. It comes from the French word *desservir*, which means "to clear away the table." Remember, the next time you ask for DESSERT you are asking to clear away the table.

Words About
Things We Wear

denim

If we use the words DENIM and DUN-
GAREES, we are using words from the
French and Hindustani languages. DENIM is
a French word, a shortened form of the
phrase *serge de Nîmes*. Nîmes is a manufac-
turing town in southern France, and serge is
a kind of cloth that was made there. *Serge de
Nîmes* became *denime*, which later became
DENIM.

dungaree

In India, the word *dungri* was the name for a coarse
woven cotton cloth that was used to make sails and
tents. Because it wore so well, sailors used it to
make work clothes, too. *Dungri,* after a time, became DUNGAREE, but the cloth is still used to
make work clothes.

corduroy

Even though it was invented in England, CORDUROY is
thought to be a French word. In France, *corde* means "cord,
rope, or line," which describes the appearance of the fabric,
and *du roi* means "of the king." According to that, COR-
DUROY means "corded fabric of the king," and the story is
that many years ago the cloth was used to make hunting
clothes for the royal families.

pajamas

Two Persian words, *pai,* meaning "leg," and *jamah,* meaning "garment," gave us our next word. *Pai-jamah,* which meant "leg garment," was the way people in the Orient used to refer to the loose trousers that they wore. Later on, *pai-jamahs* became PAJAMAS and came to mean a loose sleeping suit.

pants

Speaking of PANTS, they were once called pantaloons. Long, long ago, St. Pantaleone became the patron saint of Venice, Italy. An Italian comic character in a comedy act was named Pantalone, or Pantaloon, after St. Pantaleone. We have to assume that the actor must have worn some funny-looking PANTS in the act, because *pantaloni* became the Italian word for PANTS, or trousers. After a while, the French borrowed their word *pantalons* from the Italian, and it became our *pantaloons* or PANTS, which is what they are today.

thimble

When people sew, they often wear a THIMBLE on their finger or thumb. But where did the word THIMBLE come from? There seem to be two thoughts on how the word came into use. Some people think THIMBLE was actually a shortening and changing of the words *thumb bell.* A THIMBLE certainly looks like a little bell to put on the thumb. Other people think the word comes from the Old English word *thymel,* which means "little thumb." The next time you see a THIMBLE, see what you think.

umbrella

In some hot regions of the world, people use parasols or UMBRELLAS to protect themselves from the sun's rays. The Italian word for "shade" is *ombra*, from the Latin word *umbra*. *Ombra* became *ombrella*, then our UMBRELLA, which was used to cast shade, not to keep off the rain.

pocket

The word POCKET comes from the Norman-French *poket* —equivalent to the French word *poche*, which means a "pouch," the Icelandic word *poki*, which means a "bag," and the Middle Dutch word *poke*, which means a "bag" or "sack." Even today, in some parts of this country, a *poke* means a "bag." Gradually these words changed from the Old Norman language (which was Norse) to French to Anglo-Saxon to Middle English before the word POCKET came into use. Today, when we cook poached eggs, we're cooking the yolk of the egg in a bag, or POCKET, of the egg white.

mustache

The word MUSTACHE is a word that came to us from the Greek language, to Italian, then to French. The original Greek word *mystax* meant "upper lip," which is where MUSTACHES are found. If we say that someone is wearing a MUSTACHE on his upper lip, we are really saying that he's wearing an upper lip on his upper lip.

Words About Things We Ride

jeep

In the U. S. Army the letters *G.P.* stand for "General Purpose," and were applied to lots of equipment, including vehicles. *G.P.* sounds a bit like JEEP. Also, the comic strip "Popeye" had a little animal called Eugene the JEEP, who made the sound "jeep, jeep." So the car we know as a JEEP, which is certainly an American idea, came from two American sources: the U. S. Army and the "Popeye" comic strip.

taxicab

If we ride in a taxi, or a cab, or a TAXICAB, we'll be riding in a vehicle that kept getting its name shortened. Originally, in France, it was called a *taximètre* cab. A *taximètre* was the instrument that showed the fare due, and *cab*, short for *cabriolet*, was originally a one-horse carriage. *Taximètre* was shortened to *taxi*, leaving the word TAXICAB. Some people have shortened the words TAXICAB still further by calling the vehicles taxis or cabs. That's quite a change from *taximètre cabriolet*.

blimp

Every so often we see a BLIMP flying over a football stadium. Now, we know that BLIMPS are big bags full of gas that is lighter than air, and that they do not have a rigid skeleton or inside framework. During World War I, several varieties of these "soft" airships were tested. Since they were the limp rather than rigid type, the first one was called "A-limp," the second "B-limp," and so on. Eventually the "B-limp" model was adopted, and the term *B-limp* became simple BLIMP.

garage

A GARAGE may not be a form of transportation, but it may certainly be used to hold and protect jeeps and taxicabs. Originally the word came from the French word *garer*, meaning "to protect," or "to guard." When we think of a GARAGE as protecting and guarding a car, it somehow seems to make sense.

sled

If we ride on a SLED, we are really "sliding," which is where the word SLED got its start. Most of the cold European countries had some form of SLED in their languages: Middle Dutch was *sledde,* later Dutch was *slede,* Danish was *slaede,* and Swedish was *slede.* These words are directly related to the Anglo-Saxon word *slidan,* the Old High German *slitan,* and the Lithuanian *slidus,* which meant "to slide" and "slippery." It seems that the way to get a ride on a SLED is to slide on something slippery.

bicycle

From the Latin word *bi,* meaning "two," and the Greek word *kyklos,* meaning "wheel," we get *bi-kyklos,* which means "two wheels" and has become our word BICYCLE. The word BICYCLE was probably shortened to *bike* by the kids who use bikes. The same Latin word *bi,* added to the Latin words *centum,* which means "hundred," and *annus,* meaning "year," gives us the word *bicentennial,* or "two hundredth year."

caboose

The word for the end of a freight train is CABOOSE. But a long time ago, CABOOSE had nothing to do with trains and was not at the end of anything. CABOOSE is from the German word *camboose,* which meant the cook's cabin on board ship. Because that was where meals were prepared and sometimes eaten, the word was adapted to mean the eating and resting car for railroad crews on a freight train.

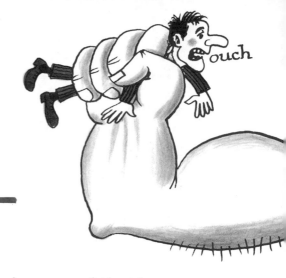

Words About
Things We Use

muscles

When we use our MUSCLES, we are using a word that has a really strange beginning. The Latin word *mus* means "mouse." The Latin word *musculus* means "little mouse." Long, long ago, when people saw MUSCLES being exercised, they must have thought those MUSCLES looked like little mice creeping around under the skin. The little mouse, or *musculus,* became our word MUSCLE.

dollars

In the year 1519, silver was first minted in a place called Joachimsthal, in Bohemia (now part of Czechoslovakia). The coins that were made were called *Joachimsthaler.* That was certainly too long a name for that money, so it was shortened to *Thaler.* The word *Thaler,* which was German, eventually became DOLLARS, which are American.

alphabet

All words are made up of letters of the AL-PHABET. But the word ALPHABET had to come from someplace, too. The Greek AL-PHABET is different from ours, and much older. It starts *Alpha, beta, gamma....* By joining together the first two letters, we got our word ALPHABET. In the Phoenician and

Hebrew languages, the first letter was *aleph*, which means "ox." Since the ox provided food, clothing, and work, *aleph*, or "ox," was most important to them. Next in importance was the second letter, *beth*, which means "house," or "shelter." *Aleph* and *beth*, combined together, was their word ALPHABET.

hatchet

When we use a HATCHET, we are using a word that is very closely related to the word *hash*. *Hash* comes from a French word *hacher*, which means "to hack or chop." But *hacher* comes from the French words *hache*, which means "ax," and *hachette*, which means "little ax." So, when we think of HATCHET, we should think of "a little ax used to chop." When we think of *hash*, we should think of "food chopped by a tool somewhat like a little ax."

album

Most photograph ALBUMS have black pages, most record ALBUMS have brightly colored pages, and most autograph ALBUMS have white or light-colored pages, yet the word ALBUM is from the Latin word *albus*, which means "white" or "blank." In ancient Roman days, a public notice would be posted on a white or blank tablet called an ALBUM, and the word came down to us to mean blank pages used to hold photographs, records, autographs, or anything else. It is from *albus* that we get the word *albino,* which means "white-skinned," and *albumen,* which is the white of an egg.

photograph

Speaking of PHOTOGRAPHS, that word comes to us from the Greek words *photo,* meaning "light," and *grapho,* meaning *"I write."* So whenever we take a PHOTOGRAPH, we are writing with light, which seems logical.

X ray

One kind of PHOTOGRAPH is an X RAY. The man who invented X RAYS, Wilhelm von Roentgen, called them *"X-strahlen." Strahlen* is German for RAYS, and because the rays he discovered were unknown to him, he called them "X," which means an unknown quantity.

drum

The word DRUM is said to be of "imitative origin." That simply means that the word sounds like what it means. It possibly came to us from the Dutch word *trom* or the earlier Middle Dutch word *tromme.* By saying those words together, *trom, tromme,* DRUM, we can certainly hear the sounds that a DRUM makes.

window

If someone tried to tell you about "an eye for the wind," you probably wouldn't know what he meant. But that's how the word WINDOW came about. In the Scandinavian languages, there was a word *vindauge,* which was made up of two other words, *vindr,* meaning "wind," and *auga,* meaning "eye." By combining "an eye to let the wind in," another word was invented.

lasso

The Spanish word *lazo* means a rope with a sliding noose at one end. This became our word LASSO. Yet many people confuse a LASSO with a *lariat,* which is from the Spanish *la reata,* meaning "the rope," and is used to tie or hobble cattle. LASSO and lariat may both be made of rope, but they have different meanings. Both words were adopted by our cowboys from Spanish cowboys and the Spanish language.

scissors

We know some words that sound like what the word means, but what about a word that looks like what that word means? In the Hungarian language, the word *ollo* means SCISSORS. Certainly the two *o*'s look like the holes for fingers, and the two *l*'s look like the blades of a pair of SCISSORS. The word SCISSOR, however, comes from ancient Rome and originally meant a "tailor" or "cutter." It's related to the old French word *cisel*, which meant "chisel."

ballot

It's easy to see how a word like *balloon* might have come from *ballon*, which was the French word for "ball," but what about the word BALLOT? Not only did BALLOT come from "ball," but a ball was once used to vote for a candidate. The Italian *balla*, meaning ball, and *ballotta*, meaning "little ball," gave us the word BALLOT. In ancient Greece, a white ball was dropped into a box to vote for a candidate, a black ball to defeat him. When we hear that someone was "blackballed," we are using this ancient phrase and its meaning. If we look back in the French language, we find that the word *boulette* means "little ball," and it is from that word that we get *bullet*, which of course is a little ball that comes out of a gun. Two words, two languages, two meanings.

magazine

When we read a MAGAZINE, most of us would not realize that the word originally came from the Arabic word *makhazin*, which means a "storehouse." *Makhazin* gave the Italians their word *magazzino,* and the French *magasin,* which means "department store" and is certainly a storehouse. Books, which are storehouses of information, were once called MAGAZINES, but now the word refers to periodical publications. Ammunition supply depots are also called MAGAZINES.

Words About
Things We Enjoy

bazaar

Two words that seem similar to some people are BAZAAR and CARNIVAL. Yet they are from different languages and have entirely different meanings. BAZAAR is a Persian word that refers to a market place or street of shops in oriental countries. It is a word we now use for a sale of various articles, usually to raise money for a club or church.

carnival

The word CARNIVAL is from the Latin, Italian, and French languages and refers to the last three days before Lent. Some people think CARNIVAL is from the Latin *carne vale,* which means "flesh, farewell." Others say it comes from *carnem,* meaning "meat," and *levare,* meaning "to remove." Either way, it is a word for the feasting just before the fasting of Lent. This period of feasting and merrymaking gave the word CARNIVAL another meaning: entertainment, side shows, and games that are held for charity or profit.

mardi gras

The very last day before Lent, and the last day of CARNIVAL, is Shrove Tuesday, or MARDI GRAS, which is French for "fat Tuesday." MARDI GRAS is celebrated in New Orleans, Paris, Rome, Rio de Janeiro, and many other cities, and many

people still think of that holiday in a "party" way without knowing its real meaning.

carrousel

When we think of chariot races and tournaments, we probably wouldn't think of a merry-go-round. But that is where the word CARROUSEL, which is another word for a merry-go-round, comes from. The Italian word *carosello* means "little chariot." Around and around, from the Italian to the French to the English, went the word CARROUSEL.

magic

Most people know that the Three Wise Men from the East were called the Magi. They might not know that the word MAGIC came from the word *Magi*. The Magi were priests from ancient Persia. Their word for fire worshiper was *magus*. *Magus* entered the Greek language as *magos*, and meant "juggler" or "sorcerer." That, in turn, became *magikos*, which referred to wizardry, and eventually became the words *magical* and MAGIC.

waltz

Thinking of going around and around brings up another word that has a strange meaning. The name of the dance known as the WALTZ comes from the German *walzen*. The word WALTZ means, very simply, to "revolve or roll about," which is certainly what some people seem to do when they are dancing the WALTZ.

rodeo

Two other words that mean "going around" are RODEO and CIRCUS. RODEO is a Spanish word that means "a going around," or "to go around," or "surround," or "a cattle ring." If you've been to a RODEO, you'll probably agree that there is a lot of "going around a cattle ring." The word RODEO is closely related to the word *rotate,* which, as you know, means to "turn around."

circus

CIRCUS came to us from the Greek and Latin languages. The Greek

word for "ring" or "circle" was *kirkos*. This became the Latin word CIRCUS, also meaning "ring" or "circle." When we refer to a "three-ringed CIRCUS," we are really saying "a three-ringed ring."

toy

We get many versions of the word TOY from the Dutch, Scandinavian, and Middle English languages. *Tuig, tuyg, tygi,* and *toi* are only a few of them. Some of the early meanings of these words are: gadgets, objects, tools, playthings, apparatus, trash, stuff, and junk. If we look in some children's toy chests, we may see some of the gadgets, objects, tools, playthings, apparatus, trash, stuff, and junk that helped bring us the word TOY.

puzzle

If we *oppose* someone, we are really cross-questioning him. If we *pose* a question to someone, we are challenging him. Both of the words *oppose* and *pose* used this way are the word cousins for the word PUZZLE. PUZZLE comes to us from the Middle English *poselen* and *poselet,* which means "to confuse, to bewilder, to make difficult." Most PUZZLES, whether they are jigsaw PUZZLES, crossword PUZZLES, or any other kind, are designed to confuse, bewilder, and make things difficult for the person doing them.

golf

As far back as 1457, the game of GOLF was mentioned as being a Dutch game. The Dutch played the game with a club and ball, but the club was called a *kolf*. The word GOLF has many word cousins. In Scottish, the word *gowf* meant to "strike at"; in Icelandic, the word *kolfr* meant the "clapper of a bell"; in Low German, *Kulf* was a "hockey stick"; and in Danish, *kolbe* meant the "butt end of a weapon." It would seem very strange today to go out to a golf course and see people playing GOLF with a hockey stick, the clapper of a bell, or the butt end of a weapon.

Words About Other Things

news

It would certainly make sense to find that the word NEWS came from the initials of the four points of the compass, North, East, West, and South, which is where NEWS seems to come from. But that is not true. NEWS is an English word that comes from *newes,* meaning "new things." That was translated from the French *nouvelles,* which is the plural of the old French word *novel,* which meant "new." The Latin word *nova* and the Greek word *neos* go further back in history, yet they both mean "things that are new."

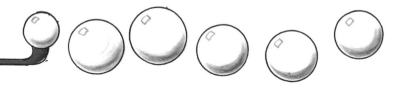

bubble

The next two words have one thing in common. They are both of "imitative origin," or words that sound like what they

mean. The word BUBBLE sounds like something bubbling, which is how the word was
invented by English-speaking people. In
Swedish, the same word is *bubbla;* in Danish,
the word is *boble;* and in Dutch the word is
bobbel. Yet they all have a bubbling sound,
and all mean the same thing.

hiccup

HICCUP, which is also spelled *hiccough,* is
another word that sounds like what it means.
Just as the word BUBBLE comes from the English language, yet is related to similar words
from other languages, so is the word HICCUP.
In French, the same word is *hoquet;* in Danish, it's *hikke;* in
Swedish, *hicka;* in Dutch, it's *hik;* in Middle Dutch, *huck-up;*
and in an old European language known as Breton, the very
same word is *hik* or *hak.*

january

The month of JANUARY got its name in an interesting way.
The Roman god Janus was the god of doors and entrances.
He was pictured as having two faces, one looking forward,
one looking back. The month of JANUARY, which takes its
name from Janus, looks forward toward the new year, and
backward at the old year. It is from this same word root that
we get the word *janitor,* who, as we know, is a doorkeeper,
and often has to look both ways to do his work.

october

OCTOBER is another month with an interesting story behind
its name. The name comes from Middle English, and from

Anglo-Saxon, all the way back to the Latin language. Since *octo* means "eight," as in *octopus,* why do you suppose OCTOBER is our tenth month instead of our eighth? Well, the answer is that it was the eighth month—in the old Roman calendar. Later, two more months were added, and when our modern calendar was adopted, OCTOBER became the tenth month even though the name means "eighth."

anniversary

When we speak of months, we often think of the word ANNIVERSARY. It comes from another Latin word, *anniversarius,* which was formed from two words, *annus,* meaning "year," and *vertere* or *versum,* meaning "to turn" or "turned." So the word ANNIVERSARY means a "turning of the year," or "returning yearly," which is exactly what an ANNIVERSARY does.

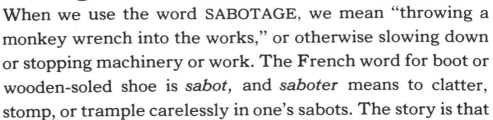

sabotage

When we use the word SABOTAGE, we mean "throwing a monkey wrench into the works," or otherwise slowing down or stopping machinery or work. The French word for boot or wooden-soled shoe is *sabot,* and *saboter* means to clatter, stomp, or trample carelessly in one's sabots. The story is that SABOTAGE meant slowing down or stopping machinery by throwing *sabots* into the works, either actually or as a figure of speech.

volcano

Two words that refer to nature's forces are VOLCANO and TYPHOON. VOLCANO is an Italian word from the Latin *vulcanus* which came from Vulcan, the god

of fire, and means "burning mountain."
This is certainly what a VOLCANO
suggests.

typhoon

TYPHOON, which is a great wind, is
thought to come from two Chinese
words, *tai* and *fong,* which mean, simply
enough, "great wind."

shampoo

SHAMPOO would hardly seem to be a
word that comes from India and Hindi
(the language of the Hindus). And yet
that is exactly where it began, as the
Hindi word *champo,* which originally
meant "to press, to knead, to squeeze, or
to wash the hair."

confetti

Sometimes at parties, people throw CON-
FETTI into the air. Originally, CONFETTI
was an Italian word and meant little candies
thrown around at carnivals and other cele-
brations. Today, little pieces of colored
paper are used in the same way.

dixie

There are two stories about how the word DIXIE came into
our language. Some think the word came from the Mason-
Dixon line, and that the land south of that line was DIXIE.

Others think it came from *dix,* the French word for "ten," printed on ten-dollar bank notes in Louisiana just before the Civil War. Either way, the land of DIXIE refers to our South. So it comes from a geographical line or the French word for ten: take your pick.

tip

Another word with two theories or stories of how it began is the word TIP, meaning something we leave after being served in a restaurant. The word is from the Middle English. This meaning, however, may have come from the abbreviation of the words "to insure promptness," which was posted on coin boxes on tables in old English coffee houses. Or it may have come from the Latin word *stips,* meaning "gift," which was related to the Latin *stipendium,* which meant "salary" or "income."

okay

If we are puzzled by a word with two theories of its origin, here is a word that has four stories of how it began, all quite different. OKAY—or OK—is an American word, and possibly came from the Choctaw Indian word *okeh,* which means "it is so." On the other hand, it might have come from an abbreviation used in early American trade and commerce, when clerks with terrible spelling marked shipments OK, meaning "orl korrect." Or it might have come from shipments of fine rum and molasses from a place known as Aux Cayes in Haiti. Aux Cayes was pronounced OK, and so the barrels were marked OK. But most people who study words and how they began think it had yet a different origin. Our eighth president, Martin Van Buren, was born in Kinderhook, New York. Kinderhook had a Democratic club in 1840, which supported him for a second term. The club was known as the "Old Kinderhook," which became shortened to OK. One word, two or four letters long—four different stories of how it began.

So there they are: 101 words—and how they began. Some of them go back to early history. Some of them come from distant lands and languages. Some of them imitate what the word means. A few of them were even mistakes that entered our language and stayed.

You may have known most of these words; maybe you knew them all. You probably didn't know how most of them came into our language.

There are people who study how words began. They are

called *etymologists*. There are also people who study language. They are called *linguists*. In a small way, by reading about these 101 words and how they began, you have become an etymologist and a linguist. You have become a student of *language*, which, by the way, comes from the Latin word for "tongue," *lingua*. You have increased your *vocabulary*, which is a "list of words."

There are people who collect *oxymorons*, which are "contradictory words or groups of words," such as *jumbo shrimp*. These people have fun looking for words that are opposite in meaning, yet are often used in our language. If *jumbo* means "large," and *shrimp* means "small," what is a *jumbo shrimp?*

Collecting and learning about words is, in a way, somewhat like collecting and learning about sea shells, or stamps, or butterflies. Except, of course, that most people don't put collections of words on shelves, or frame them and hang them on walls. Yet a collection of words goes with us wherever we go; it can grow and be strengthened every time we talk with someone; and it can help us in one of the most important things in life: communicating with others.